Conscious Energy

ISBN 978-1-948613-17-0

Library of Congress Control Number: 2022913805

Sunny Day Publishing, LLC
Cuyahoga Falls, Ohio 44223
www.sunnydaypublishing.com

Printed in the United States of America

Conscious Energy

Poems by Daniel Dischino

Artwork by Elizabeth Amigo-Dischino

Photos by Elizabeth Amigo-Dischino
and Daniel Dischino

Chapters

Acknowledgements

I would like to acknowledge and thank allpoetry.com, especially the Late Night Poets group, for their inspiration.

Kelonie Utley, LeeAnn Roberts, Rachel Walker, Megan Kelsey, and Scott Sharpe for their collaboration and motivation.

My parents, Arthur and Mary Dischino, may they Rest In Peace, for their dedication to providing my sister Ellen and I with a wonderful foundation.

I hope this book brings all readers true elation as much as it did to me during its creation.

Peace and happiness

This book is dedicated to
my beautiful wife Elizabeth
and son Daniel
to which also everything I do is dedicated
Once a loving family one has,
there is no other want or reason.

Humanity

I am invisible
As the world sees what it wants
When all I want
Is to be a part
of the world again
All I want from humanity
Is to be seen as human

I am legacy

Seems so long ago
and it seems like yesterday.
A time when dreams were my definition
but I cannot place the moment
when I woke
Why do dreams fade so fast
I know I have had them
I know I still do
but where did they go?
I used to fly over the hills
to see what was on the other side
now I'm not sure if I can make it to the top
what a fool I was to chase those dreams
as they are always destined to fade
As to fade is my destiny awaiting
What of memories soon to be buried
What of my song that dissipates in the wind
Why do I hunger so for the passion of the fleeting
moment
when I can join the immortals with the power of legacy
The fleeting passions of a laborer long to dust
is but a lost drop of rain
compared to the reservoir which he built that still
hydrates today
What have I done!
I listened to the philosophy of the now
when in truth there is no now
Children of the future will not hear my sorrow
for the reaping I have done
so I must use God's gift of redemption
and grasp onto that mythical now

as my gateway to immortality.
Why write a coda
that no one will hear
when I can start the overture of generations
for generations of eons to come
I am dust
or I am Legacy
I will not let fate choose
when I have the ultimate power of choice
I am immortal
I am legacy

The tragedy of mind

What tragedy of mind will haunt me today

Which part of the fool am I destined to play

I shelter in place with my arrogant lies

that dominate thoughts under factual guise

All facts can't be criminal some must be correct

But which can I trust and which are suspect

This puzzle of mine brings me close to insane

in a world so elusive with a mind so in pain

A poor mental scribe I wander the land

A new world each day to misunderstand

I think myself brave with my journey of age

but knowledge and wisdom share a similar stage

The enemy may tear the unfamiliar apart

but true evil prays on what is dear to my heart

I grasp all I know through the evolved gift of senses

in a world cruelly made with undetectable fences

My eyes to perceive but only after it's gone

My ears only hear once the sound is withdrawn

Taste, just a prisoner of cravings tight clutch

And feel just a myth of the illusion of touch

Am I able to fix this cruel lifelong delusion

or is delusion itself my only conclusion

The only tool that I have to fix of what I have spoken

Is the very same tool that I have tragically broken

And I am not sure if I should take comfort or shame

In the fact that I'm human

and we are all the same

Starship wandering

I walk alone amidst the many

I've walked before with many more

By moonlit skies on quiet nights

through city streets with blazing lights

searching always searching

for what, I know not for

With the future always lurching

like a knock up on my door

Endless paces, familiar places under endless watchful skies

With a message always sending from the song that sings

unending

Unending as the birdsong that responds in a reprise

A song I barely hear

as I walk throughout the year

Searching always searching

for what

I know not for

Endless cycle of rhythm and rhyme

meter and motion, the music of time

A verse that's soon forgotten

Lost in human lore

A ship of fools ever sailing

They walk the deck ever wailing

walking, ever walking

Searching aimlessly for shore

Ship of fools in an endless sea

there floats the path of humanity

Song of the titans

And I wander these lonely streets
Through the madness of the movement
With the accord of the machinery
And I take in the energy of the moment
The pulse, the rhyme, the rhythm, the time
Urban winds singing a symphony
Metal and mortal voices merge in harmony
To announce a voice that speaks to me

Far away from the rush and the race
I walk through a long forgotten place
In an aria so silent, so perfectly awake
A composition more than a billion years to make
I have found my source I have found my dawn
I connect and I breathe before it's gone
For want and greed for this we trade
For pride and need for what we made

And I walk the path through the cool silent air
Past the waving grass in the sun-colored sky
A bird ride the winds and the sun shows my way
And the bird sings to me with an alluring cry

A house in the distance near the road to town

By a windy stream with trees all around

My focus acute as you race from your chair

The allure of your step and the breeze through your hair

I feel the light

I feel the life

I feel the drive

I feel alive

Armchair quarterback

Beware the temptation of judgment
Voice of the fool
The quicker the judgment
the more foolish the judge

Lost at sea
I truly am
not the fluid oceans of earth
not the deep ocean void of space
but the vast ocean of numbers
I am but one

somewhere between the one and the infinity
lost somewhere

14 billion years of existence
Yet I scratch and claw through 100
barely conscious of my surroundings

100
100 billion travelers
100 billion scribes
With 100 billion stories
how many have I read?
I'm too busy writing down my own

I dive in to see how deep the numbers go
a few precious building blocks
That's everything
how much can there be?

I read, ponder, observe, and study
Library after library, book after book
Humbled
a walk to clear my mind
but I can't hide
I look and listen
and all I see is different
that tree is different from that tree
that house is different from that house
that bird sounds different than that one
to the familiar surroundings of my home
I retreat
defeated
I can't know it all

The dream of wisdom is dead
praise the wonder of discovery

Young man barely out of school
embarks to take a world to rule
All will bow to serve his might
he knows it all, he knows he's right
the rest of us to him a fool
His shadow fades, in the rising light

The beauty of balance

Darkness holds the hidden adventures of the unlighted path
The illusion of darkness is dependent on the reliance of light
Can humanity only thrive from outside illumination?
For reliance on the light clouds the illumination of wisdom
But I am human
Blind me and I will see through the eyes of memory
Deafen me and I will hear you through your actions
Back away from me and I will grasp onto you with the power
of the spoken word
I will not succumb to any singularity
I will laugh at defeat with the power of connection

Hail the almighty corpus callosum!

Darkness an annoyance in the pursuit of the unknown
I am human
I have created light
With the delicate flip of a
switch
darkness is defeated
unable to penetrate the might which I have created

But alas, humbling reality is a persistent foe
as an avalanche to level mountains

is only snowflake away

And word switch itself uses its duality to relieve me of my
power with even the gentlest rain
to switch the dominance and
extinguish the light of man

Curse evolutions joke of arrogance and ego, the enemy of the
wise
For the true nature of light reveals what I have created
a gentle balance with the darkness
illumination into the unknown
An invitation into the mysteries of nature
I must learn to not overstay my welcome

Age

As I see the world through history's eyes

I feel the years of experience that have defined my own

existence

Culture permeates

dominates

infects

molds the open mind

controls the week

fascinates the curious

tattoos the experiences

and mystifies those who came before and those who are to

come

We all live through history, but not all experience it

Each generation a window into the stories of their time

Tales of the past, once reality

Dreams of the future, an unstoppable destiny

The open mind easily travels through time using the lost art

of listening

I reach out to the elders, alone and forgotten, to understand
the wisdom of the reason why

I hear the voices of youth, undervalued and ignored,

to peer into the future and see the sparks of brilliance ignite

I feel the harmony of all generations in the tolerant and the
humble

And I see the wise become enlightened at the realization of
the insignificance of the difference of age

Marble cries

Forgotten legends of a forgotten people
Forest shadows on the desert sand
History etched in waves of rock
Grain after grain of memory
shifting with each sandstorm
carrying the thunder of battle drums
pounded with hollow bones
and felt with each step I take
in the wind ruled canyons of city streets

Far away beyond my sight
A hawk dives, a meteor to the ground
to grab a mouse
and let the others scurry off

Distant cries of falling might, echo through museum halls
Marble and bronze propaganda warriors
stand ghostly white
trapped in earthly memories
from altered realities
on murdered forests
sold for meditative comfort
I dream in words, of foundations end
but screams of marble ghosts drown the music of greatness
past

I walk alone through shaded fields
1000 ants beneath my feet
returning home from victory
They've marched before and will again

A maze of glass steel and rock
the heavy weight of mankind
to push the past deep below the earth
A tower of babel on every street corner
Battle drums echo from passing cars and open windows
Songs of conquest echo in the movement of every man
and trumpets of victory echo in the construction site
symphonies like marble cries through museum nights

A sparrow flies over all
to land on a statue
in a busy summer park
he waits

Survey of a cult leader

Power
Unlike other types of greed I see no end
No satisfaction, no rest, no height to ascend
Lust, money, and adoration in a branded tower
Pawns in my quest for unlimited power
My initial appearance creates a moral defiance
Repetition, my weapon, brings a growing compliance
I promise hope, success, a welcoming change
Only fanatical devotion I ask in exchange
Those that defy me you can easily see
Are suddenly pure evil, on this we agree
Come worship at my counsel wise women and men
As I declare my glory again, and again, and again
And my words are pure truth, to be praised, amen
This I tell you again, and again, and again
It all makes sense to you why didn't it then
I just needed your thoughts again, and again, and again
You understand me now you do not need to know why
No more need to entice no more need for a hook

Doubters are heretics persistent with lies
I too now believe
I have seen myself reflecting in the righteous army
The ultimate power of control
Unconditional control for the promise of truthful freedom
Question and perish, surrender and be free

This is all I ask

The power of control, I am, I become

Of the body

Of what gift is greater than thy own self
of what tool is greater that man can make then man
The surveyor of worlds
The reflector of music
The devourer of energy
The grasper of all within reach
Unending input with unending processing
The pleasure of life at the whim of thought
Asleep are those
who do not see the world before them
who only hear and do not listen
who touch but do not connect
and who do not seek to understand
Trapped are those
who are a slave to passion and cannot truly enjoy
who devour for greed and not to nourish or protect
And truly lost are those
who absorb without contemplation
who answer without question
and who sense without wonder
The path for them is long forgotten
Of what greater connection to the stars than the stardust
within
What greater power to wield than the atomic we are
What better for the spirit to steer with than the mind
and what greater vessel to journey to the eternal in
than us

The race

Let the race of men beware and take cover from the race of man
For as the focus of inner selfless grows with each desire
the inevitable explosion will flood the world with a sea of anger
and greed
So easy is the self
for it takes no vision
even a blind man can see what is inside even a deaf man can hear
his own voice
And even those numb to the world can feel their own cravings
As all are born equal, and end equal
as we race through the cosmos
For dust is dust and all blows equally in the wind
So in a race where all finish
and all prizes are the same
would a wise man not walk with his fellow racers to enjoy the
journey as one
and laugh at the fool who runs alone?
A fool who runs a race he doesn't understand
A fool who is tired and weak at the end
A fool who took no notice of the race itself
or the track on which he ran
A fool who looks back at the competition
only to question why they are smiling

So beware the self in selfish

for it poisons the mind with greed

And beware the self in selfless

for the righteous take no pleasure in your suffering

But rejoice in the unity of ourself

and walk together as one

Words

Of the lives we touch
of the power that each word wields

A secret chat with a bonded mate
The "Thank you" of a Stranger on a crowded street
Tell me the difference

So guarded are the words I let in
how guarded are the words I let out?
Words of power, words of passion
words of intellect, and words of innocence
words to cause wars above all other weapons
words to comfort and heal amidst all wars

I think so hard, for years sometimes, on words that penetrate
my skin
Yet how quickly are the words I shout, a weapon from within

In the quiet evening
After the chaotic energy of the sun
has let me be
As my demons release into the night

I stand free and peaceful

to wish upon thoughts

Oh universe from which I came

please give me an armies strength

Not the strength to attack

but the strength to refrain

Please give me a scholars intellect

not to understand within

but to help those without

Please give me the magic of a wizard

not to distort nature

but to display a sense of wonder to others

And please bring me back to my animal roots

like the noble birds who have conquered the third dimension

Not like a hawk who's power is spent on innocent prey

but like the wild dove

who is beauty and joy

and brings hope to all who behold

And who's mere silhouette

brings a symbol of peace to mankind

Faith ends strife

Faith is health

Faith is life

Faith gives wealth

Common ground

A message for my sisters and brothers

I have seen this world as heaven and hell

And to those who want to be the others

We are moving on and wish you well

Another message for those in pain

You are part of the nation of man

And the only thought that should remain

That peace for all is the only plan

You know me and I know you

This is truth, we are the same

Yet some are blind to what is true

As fools will light the world aflame

But still I see what gives me faith

As peace and love do sail abound

To fight against the hateful wraith

And lift us up before we're drowned

Have faith that reason is still around

Have faith reason is the dominant sound

Know thoughtful reason can still be found

to create a peaceful garden on our common ground

Regret

I am the darkness I have become.

I am temptations slave.

So far from home I have traveled.

The return path lost to dust.

I should've climbed over the mountain that lay before me

instead of giving into the shadows below.

Lost within

so far removed from the light

I claw at my skin

desperation to be set free

but I only find pain and blood.

I once was light

but I am now lost in the tunnels of darkness.

Please all merciful universe

free me from the mountain

which I am under so deep

and give me one ray of light

to show me the way.

Of adulthood

With the wings of a butterfly
I am propelled by cyclonic hurricane breath

At the mercy of each gentle zephyr and every terrorizing
thunderbolt
each flutter of wing a passing memory
and an additional confusing line in the encyclopedia of
infinite knowledge

I let the hands of time carry me over jagged mountains and
burning deserts
and I remember those long journeys of survival during quiet
moonlit nights

I cherish each magic filled meadow and welcoming field,
that I find to rest upon
Each soft flower petal that protects and nurtures is a moment
of perfection

Oh on what a wondrous playground do I frolic and run

with painted shades of green and blue

I fall and cry, I laugh in the sun

While days in school do shatter true

An infant in the infinitesimal

We are all children

Always

The lost key

Of what does build the human cage
but the bounty of which we reap
And where is the key but hidden within
buried under years of thought
Thought of gathered knowledge
Knowledge of unorganized experience
Experience unfiltered through ignorance
Ignorance unprotected by innocence
Innocence lost
in times unforgiving void

What strength does a mere human have
of what tools to find the long lost key

I can resist anything
except temptation
so temptation I will eliminate
I can only crave
my desires
so I will desire nothing
I can only hate
the ones I despise
so I will conquer hate

I can learn to understand all that I comprehend

and I can not comprehend only what I don't understand

So I will question what I know

And I will first learn to understand the question

And of the lost key?

I will learn from regret

and only regret if I have not learned

There is another way out

Onward!

Hope

I am invisible
As the world sees what it wants
When all I want
Is to be a part
of the world again
All I want from humanity
Is to be seen as human

The always of a new beginning

How cruel are the haunting mistakes of humanity's past
not as cruel as the hope of righteousness
What joy is there in the beginning with a destiny of mortal
sin
in a world where action is forever and time abandons all
behind
never to return
Time is a horde of wondering pilgrims in pursuit of the
horizon
a horizon in constant motion
spinning from illumination to darkness with moments of
twilight
Chase for the light or dark
the horde spins in circles

The straight path
a never-ending cycle of darkness and light
Exhausted and dizzy from the rhythm of existence
I stop to ponder
and watch my caravan disappear
in the future
chained to the bonds of time

Freedom with the choices I make

Caged to the choices 've made

Defeated by past beginnings

Elated by the promise of new ones

I can never start over but I can always start again

Onward once more into the horizon

Hope

There is really only one word,
for there is nothing without hope

I have faith in humanity
and I have had faith destroyed by treachery
as faith is in a moment where hope is everlasting

I know love is the reason
but what is love without the hope of perpetuity and truth

I have seen my own selfishness of youth turn to the
selflessness of family
I know of a family's motivation for the hope of longevity

I feel life's grandeur of enlightenment amplify with each
piece of knowledge that reveals an image of wisdom
Yet life becomes stagnant when missing the hope of purpose

We are drive, we are passion, and we are thrust into the
future never reaching the target, never stopping to rest
Who are we if not our own story
What aspirations can we have if not our own legacy

Certainly not fleeting moments of enjoyment

Truly not the greed of collection or the unending passion of experience

For the goal of satisfaction is a dangerous path

The lone carnivore whose purpose is to consume, is doomed to be lost in history

But the volcano whose brief but explosive existence of giving itself to the world, can leave an island in the vast oceans of emptiness

I will become hope or I will become nothing

The power of prayer

What a torturous fate I have found

locked away in the prison of thought

For how wonderful is the dream of grasping the stars

diamonds for the taking just overhead

each night another chance

until the thought of how

unleashes the destroyer of all dreams:

The awakening to reality

And the stars become a distant spark long since gone

Why bring me from the safety of the trees

so blessed with fruit and birdsong

only to land on the cold hard earth

where both fruit and bird fade to dust

How can I be so plagued with questions with the only cure,

the sadness of answer

So tired from the demands of life

so frightened by the voice of death

I sleep to hide

I walk to escape

I dream to dream

and I live for the moments between life

Enticed by the gift of pleasure only to be captured as a slave

by desire

Drawn to a mystical mountain summit by wonder

only to witness the fragility of the world

an avalanche only a snowflake away

Prostrate I fall to the ground

the tears of human desperation cloud my vision

and I am lost in prayer begging for universal mercy

What is this vision that has blessed my mind's eye? Has the

torture of reality become the enlightenment of truth?

Am I just an infant in evolutions plan, crying and helpless

with moments of pure wonder?

Wait!

Just a flicker in time

like a sparkle of sunlight from the first drops of spring rain

So glorious is the heavenly light of wisdom

that I now understand the reason behind the journey

through painful knowledge

I am saved by the power of true heart driven prayer

with a simple answer

There is hope

God's message

How beautiful is mornings sweet embrace
The gentle touch of sunlight to awaken the world with
warmth and color
I breathe the days first breath and watch the curtains grow
brighter with each minute
creating curiosity of what lies beyond

impossible to comprehend may be the heavenly and the
eternal
impossible to not wonder
if the renewal of sleep is not a message from God
to start us off each day with those first few precious
moments of calm and peace

Yesterday's sorrow forgotten in dream
Future anxiety yet to be released from its cage
The mind clear and pure
open to the endless possibilities of what awaits
Every day the message is clear
Today I will listen

The war of today

As I admit defeat from a restless night
the frailness of humanity dominates
Immortal in youth, the reckless mind conquers all
Mortal with age, the wise mind understands
Experience grows the warriors strength
Wisdom armors the weakening body

Weary from 10,000 days of psychic attacks, praying for
10,000 more
Each day to rise from the trenches and face the enemy with
grace, passion, and hope
Each attack grows weaker for I've seen them all before
And the path through the crossfire and trap hidden earth
grows brighter with each moment in motion and longer with
each cowering hesitation
For fate waits for no one
And each breath of wind once gone is lost to the horizon

So cast your fate into the wind and let the challenges of the
day become the triumphs of tomorrow
And day after day build your fortress high
Each triumph another brick

Each restful moment of reflection another layer of mortar to connect them all

Until the war has ended

Until the enemy, unable to penetrate the fortress of your will, turns away powerless and defeated

A small moment on the journey

The days blur and the nights blend
In the past I could see the future, but now that I'm here, I am consumed
by the past

Unable to reach beyond each moment
I know there is brightness ahead, but my eyes are consumed by shadows
Blinded by knowledge
Deafened by sound
Numbed by experience
The peace of innocence lost a lifetime ago
All this knowledge gathered through the years like pieces of a puzzle
The harder I try to complete the puzzle, the more pieces I gather
Confidence turns to confusion
A purposeful mission curves uncontrollably

The path lost in time

Time
Why do I always forget
Time is always the answer, there is really no choice
As I head into the shadows, time sees me through
As I am, as I become lost in distress, time pushes on with the rhythm and
the pulse of good times and bad
I will wait, prepare, and embrace the only true concern
What's next

The dream of Herodotus

I am the future
I am of what ancients did dream
I am the future's past
A whisper where there once was a scream

I am a traveler in both time and space
the foot prints of a soon forgotten place

To those who will not see the dawn
I hold the torch to carry on

And to those with whom the future lies
grasp the day before it dies
for time waits not for compromise
it only waits for our demise

So grasp hold of life and do not wait
For soon you stand at Heaven's Gate
Do not believe in rigid fate
Attack the day before it's too late

The Traveling Monk

The quest continues
The quest is always moving
forward
It is the quester that stops

Of distance

I walk the streets to a store up ahead
In a few moments I'll be there
Right now I am not
The store is as far as the moon
until I am there

The moon
hangs in the sky
as far away as the plane
that flies below it
to my reach

What is a woodland walk on a summer morning to a prisoner
What is a glass of water across the room to the bed ridden
What is one yard to a quarterback
What is an inch to a seal escaping the jaws of a shark
What is Andromeda to the Milky Way

What is distance but a connection unmade
and what is the meaning of connection
when everything is part of the everything

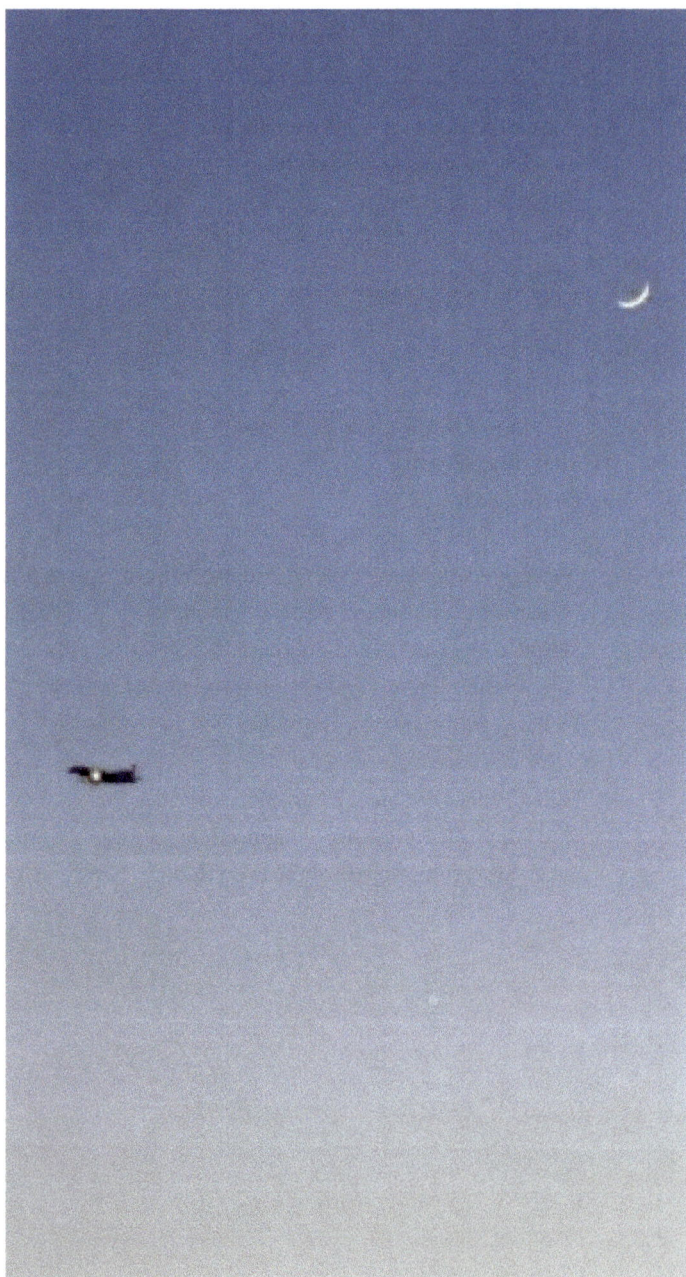

Question everything

I really don't know how to be right

I just know how to be me

I always try to follow the light

but am I blinded by what I see

How wrong I was about so many things

How can I know I'm right now

Am I just a puppet pulled by fateful strings

or am I the puppeteer in control somehow

What if I'm wrong, what if I fail

What if I'm false in the next thing I say

I must be strong I'm not this frail

or maybe I am, at least today

But the truth is out there, there has to be truth

We can't all be wrong, but I guess we can't all be right

Am I wiser now or was I wiser in youth

Am I scared to be wrong or am I just scared of fright

I must travel with hope and stick to the plan

to question and always question to learn

I just have to try the best that I can

Alone in dreams of remembrance

A demand calling from something ancient, something primitive
Takes me out of the safety and security that I have built
On a quest that the journey is the destination
The ambition is not the arrival but the completion
Pavement, stone, grass, and soil become one with endless promise
Meditating on movement, fixating on the future path
I see birds perched on tree and wire
Unaware of which one has not always been
Rival wanderers past introspective and steadfast
as a reflection offering, an unemotional affirmation
Insignificant and common I am quickly lost in the unforgiving memory
Cars move hastily, unaware of my resolute quest
as if I am fused with the surroundings
A plane in the silent distance distracts my contemplation while I am
unable to reciprocate
Adrift alone and invisible in an expanse of mobility and action
Advancement a flexible continuum
With a myriad of visionary curiosities displayed, a glance at the unending
path announces a mystery
Foot prints trapped in cement betray a forgotten expedition
No evidence of intent, no sign of origin
A durable secretive testimony to a mirroring adventure
Leaving no impression and covered in the disguise of the mundane,
I proceed home
My journey vanished to history and scattered in the dreams of remembrance

Who am I

Who am I

A question I might not want to know

yet here I am

cursed with contemplation

attacked by unrelenting thought

I grow so weary of the battle

and pray for mercy

from the truth of which I seek

Truth I am hoping will guide my path

For all paths lead to death

but not all paths are the same

Which one is correct?

All creatures walk the path

but not all creatures know why

or know where they are going

But death cannot define me

For it is a shared fate

and in the now, I am life

I am flesh and bone

I am heart and blood

I am breath and carnage

I am every creature to walk the earth

I am mind, I am body

I am desire, and I am peace

I am water, I am rock

I am earth, and I am fire

I am made from the stars

and I am born from the oceans

I am one billion years in the making

And I am a flash in the illumination of time

I am everything

I am all

But alas

what I have found is everyone

I am no different than every other mortal being

Where has this all taken me

perhaps back to the beginning

back to the question

who am I

within the question itself might just be the answer

Who am I?

I am

Perception

To dream, to awake, to dream

What wonders the mind unveils

Visions of futures trapped in the unconscious

Distorted perceptions of sensibility

Outlandish stories in a paralyzed state

Or a ceaseless bombardment of responsive enlightenment

Limitless possibilities for direction from reflection

with the impossible obstruction of previous experience

Innocence the lone dispassionate window of truth

Innocence distorted towards oblivion with every instant

Everything is genuine, everything is deceptive

The skies protect with the guardians of the gods

and age into a vast cold emptiness

I feel the energy I've stolen to fuel my flight

I drink the water that fueled the origins of life

I see the light of the world and wonder it's fate

I see the emptiness deep within all things

I see all and I see nothing

A moment in Time

An early cold January night

Dressed in a coat, hat, and gloves provided by fortune

and family, I venture out into the dark still air, away from

comfort and security

Coat secured and headphones assured I find warmth in

motion and music, meditating on songs from my antiquity

The silent streets now belong to me, each car and fellow

explorer becomes an invader in this tranquil music narrated

painting that I have entered

Time and environment forgotten amidst the meditation of

music, movement and streetlights

The journey becomes a continuous composition with no

beginning, no end, no memory, and no meaning

After a lost shadow of time, I find myself in a familiar place

One of safety and belonging

Yet I hesitate at its entrance in the now exhilarating and

refreshing primal air

Every breath an invigorating sense of triumph

Silent clouds sail by like ships in the darkest of nights during

the calmest of seas.

Over the hibernating trees and rooftop silhouettes,

and beneath attentive stars,

a plane flies calmly, off to the distance

Its soft lambent lights blending with the night

Altogether creating a unique impression that I, alone at this

moment, in this place, can see

Never before known to man

Never to be seen again

I migrate inside to the warmth of home and family

A pearl in the void

What paths will carve from travelers' tales
Dancing spirits on a questing flight
as the flow of blood on city streets
or a hidden path over woodland hills
when come to meet forgotten seas
A call to sail, to wind submit
to float above the darkened depths
to sway upon the dancing waves
and cross the void to distant lands
between two oceans
to crash the shore

What pilgrims walk on beaches made
of comet dust by waters blade
We stare above on starry nights
and ponder space between the lights
Till morning brings the Sun's command
to shine like pearls on glistening sand
Each grain of sand of earth reflects
a pearl to be if fate directs

What cosmic explorers may sail the void
and search for treasures in the sea of lights
Among the floating rocks and dust
a pearl of blue and green invites

Quest

Wandering
a monk made of flickering light
trapped in a cage of flesh
searching for emptiness with the hope of universal truth
A knight on a quest, one in an endless series of long forgotten knights
But what of the quest
Cruel is the fate of the curious who race toward the end and forget the
journey
How can a quester know the direction if they do not know what they seek
How can the thinking mind solve a puzzle when the pieces are hidden by
thought
The clear mind holds the key to open the doors of enlightenment
Yet I cannot see the message written by the stars when obscured by clouds
I cannot see the colors of the horizon when the fog from an ocean breeze
overtakes
And I cannot hear the calming rhythm of a train in the distance when the
rain washes it away
Time has punished me with a mind of memories
and left clarity but a dream lost in a thousand painful dreams
And I have seen too much pain not to feel
And I have heard the splash of too many fallen tears not to have the cries of
the saddened echo endlessly in the soundtrack of those dreams
But clarity must exist
As obscured would not be a word if there was not something beyond
The quest continues
The quest is always moving forward
It is the quester that stops
I will keep moving
I will take the next step
How can I not

Love

The stars look down
They look at you
When they look at me
They wish
For I can touch heaven

I remember

I remember what you said to me in the tall grass so long ago
I remember
We left all behind
we needed it not
We set off for ancient hills with mythical stories
it was a destined path

I remember what you said

I remember the healing wind dancing within your hair
and the swaying grass mirrored with jealous reflection
I remember the shine in your eyes, the envy of the sky
And I remember the happiness in your smile that charmed
the sun itself to shine a little brighter on our day

A gift of purpose from the gods
A torn page for a long lost fairytale
When I am lost in the mayhem
When I am trapped in darkness
I think back on that smile that ignited the sun
Proof that some magic flows eternal

I remember what you said to me in the tall grass so long ago
I remember it with each morning's kiss

Forever

What of the rose that a valentine brings
compared to a rose that flowers each spring
A sweet tender moment does holiday's kiss make
but never as sweet as each mornings kiss when we wake
The soft gentle sound of your heavenly voice
like a song of the angels when the heavens rejoice
The grace of your touch like a gentle spring shower
ignites burning embers of my passionate power
I live for these times when we are together
And hope time has no end, unless it's forever

Free love

The growing years accelerate the childhood race
To release maternal bonds and grasp freedoms embrace
As the adventurous call from a strong inner voice
longs for an answer from unforgiving choice
And I'm soon to discover as freedom awakes
That the freedom of choice binds to the choices one makes
Still I cannot ignore the passion I feel
And I choose the excitement of freedom's appeal

Free to conquer all that I see
Free to explore the limits of me
Free to submit to loves siren cries
and the joy and pain that love amplifies

And in all of the years and with all of the choices
Only when captive by love the heart truly rejoices
For my freedom led quest brought me finally to see
When truly in love, it's no more about me

A peaceful passion

I absorb all of my surroundings
an antenna for spirits wandering in the flesh
the love, the pain, the torment, and the joy
static in the airwaves of contemplation
I feel the anger of the world and I am frightened and defensive
I feel the sadness of the world and I am motivated yet helpless
I feel the passion of the world and I am energized yet tormented
only in solitude is there relief
deep in the covers with a book or a song
late night walk, dancing between shadows
or a quiet Sunday afternoon, meditating on daily chores
Then does the energy radiate outward
Then does tension melt in the sunshine
Then does the peace of self delight
Then do thoughts of you ignite
Your eyes, the light of entrancing desire
Your kiss, the power of earthly conquest
Your touch, the spark to set the world ablaze
Your skin, the feel of Heaven's Gate

Two souls at peace, two souls unite
Not hindered by a human plight
Entangled love of bonds so tight
We own the night till mornings light

Love can wait

She speaks to me in tears
and in tears I answer
Bodies may touch, but minds connect
lust is craving, love is knowing

That first glance that brought me her beauty
held no longing
as destiny is an assured path

A kiss to give lights a selfish flame
but a kiss to get lights the spark eternal

The thief who steals his treasure in the night
must always hide it in shame and fear
but the gift received brings forever joy
to display on the mantelpiece of one's true character

I was confused by the loves that were wrong
but knew at first glance of the love that was right

And the part of me that I did not know was broken
was fixed in an instant
The difference between a kiss of lust and a kiss of love

To awake when she awakes
to be strong when she's weak
to accept without thought
to have comfort without question

The gates of paradise are two
side-by-side
loves reward for patience and respect

Home

I speak not of the cold brick and dead wood that cages me
It is the home I have found in the warmth and longing I feel in your embrace
And it is thoughts that comfort me when you leave
Not thoughts of sadness
for you are too kind to leave that as your parting gift
But thoughts of remembrance
A memory of the first glimpse of angelic beauty I found on this harsh cruel world
A vision sent for me alone
A memory of the first time our lips touched
how can I forget, they have never unlocked
And mostly not a remembrance but a continuum
A constant elation ignited from the first time I held you as we slept
Unable to get close enough
Magnetic forces beyond attraction
A feeling past the carnal and the comfort
one I still cannot describe today
except as peace and belonging
Home
But even those words do not convey the sense of elation I felt
with the treasure I found
that I did not know I was looking for
How can one describe a true connection
not a connection made, but a connection that has always been
A discovery of purpose entwined with the fate of the heavens expressed in the bliss of happiness
Happiness unbreakable
and as you leave you turn with a wave and a kiss
I smile
not because I know that you will return home
but because I know you will bring home back to me

Belonging

Embrace me as I weep
Calm me as I rage
For in the magic of your touch, all is lost and forgotten
An insatiable passion, you and I disappear into the one
Everything I have, everything I have done
is gone with one gentle touch
and there is only you
I know there is a world
but I can only see your eyes
I know there is music
but I can only hear your pleasure
I escape time's mortal grasp
and feel the pulse of eternity
as hours become seconds
and the fate of age becomes the power of youth
Consumed by entanglement, senses blend into desire
time is defeated, meaningless
With a deep rhythmic connection our universes collapse
Morphed from controlled motion to the welcoming chaos of
rebirth and creation
How can uncontrolled emotion and desire end in the peace of contentment?
What happens when you achieve beyond need?
What is the distance between attraction and longing?
What is beyond the ever-fluctuating restrictions of love?
Understanding does not matter
Comprehension means nothing
Reason has no purpose
I know only the peace created by our energetic embrace
I feel only the sense of belonging in your entanglement
Beyond lust and love is the true meaning of home I have found
within your arms

Journey to Forever

Angelic radiance in a mortal form
A vision sent deep within for my eyes only
How could the rest of the world be so blind
when the light of beauty was so strong
A light that gave clarity to my everything
as the world suddenly made sense
Beyond the burning of desire
I felt the peace of purpose
A sign pointing to my true path where the destiny of love awaited
Such a moment of pure enlightenment for a mere child of loves grace to
experience
I only needed to wait until our first fated kiss
your hands grabbed mine so tight
I touched your face
And I let the bond of your eyes grasp hold
and I held the universe in my hands
all else disappeared
I have found a discovery beyond value
a discovery you cannot seek
That only one chance will deliver
The revelation that the path of love is not the destination
but the journey
and that the adventure the journey holds, is as seen through the eyes of
the traveling partner
The days of wonder we travel merge into a continuum of years
only to return to the memory of days
Days of joy, days of sorrow
Days of passion, days of pain

Yet I am still that child who witnessed the angel so long ago
He seems so far gone
but it is still me

Only wiser from the journey
Only wiser to the true message from heaven
For what are angels if not to bring us on a journey to Heaven
Not a journey within filled with earthly possessions destined for dust
or memories lost in the void of experience
for now the clarity in which I saw and the purpose in which I was given
has become the truth to the paths end
For my love be not a guide
but a connection to the keys of paradise
found in the unity of two entangled hearts
The keys to the gates of heaven found by the guiding hand of my angel
of love
When we merge as one
into the forever

In dreams

With breathless voice
and sleepless night
thoughts of you
in dreams Ignite
A vision clear
from blinded site
of you aglow
loves delight

A distance will
of longing make
what dreams become
a chance to take
tender touch
enraptured kiss
attend the thought
of who I miss

And dreams I grasp
Before there gone
with fading night
into the dawn
The morning light
those dreams forsake
But real they turn
as we awake

Her passion invigorates

Sunlight calls through windows glow
the world awaits from dreams facade
A thought of you
I turn and smile
The light of truth
penetrates from your eyes
A summer wind
refreshes from your breath
Flowers caress
from your touch
Skin as soft
as a warm spring rain
A smile
to which the heavens float
The world within
a love embrace

Close enough, I cannot get
Deep enough, I cannot feel
One is two
and two is one

Time is powerless and stops with envy
Stars shine in the bright morning sky
I awake to reality
and I am now awakened
A spirit of peaceful energy
harmonizing with the universal tone
A day for the taking awaits

Mornings kiss

In the early morning crossroads where dreams and reality meet

that's when I think of you to bring me back home

I open my eyes to see only yours

And the world disappears and shines deep within

A gentle touch on your face to caress your cheek

and my fingers move to your lips

Lips softer than the rose petals of spring in a bright summer field

my hand moves through your hair to grab hold

To pull you close for a kiss to ignite today

A kiss of pure fire in a world of drowning rain

A kiss of enduring passion untouched by time

A kiss to bring meaning to life

I kissed to bring life to life itself

I kiss that ends with the purest of smiles

and an angelic voice with a good morning wish

The day is mine for the taking

Awakened Dreams & Revelations

of what miracles do I miss each day
that pass through my eyes

Voice of the sun

What magic the sunlight does reveal
what wonders the lights of heaven bring
Secrets the darkness will conceal
revelations my eyes joyfully sing

But what if I looked beyond mere human sight
To decipher the message brought to me by the light

For the sun calls the world with a greeting each day
To awaken the birds who sing and fly
As nocturnal creatures come out to play
when the sun sets to tell the birds goodbye

and the warm summer sun starts a kind conversation
with the welcoming flowers as they open and smile
While the trees will begin their long hibernation
When the soft autumn sun changes course for a while

Now the flora will show one more revelation
with magical color that beams so bright
When the sunlight ends it's white light migration
to explode from reflection for my eyes delight

And finally a river does now catch my eye
to bring me much closer to skyward insight
As the suns reflection shows the stars in the sky
to reveal to the world, the heavens true might

Drifter

Darkness reveals the enlightenment of the infinite
and the daylight is blinding to those that look

Alone
in an overcrowded world
Explorer on a sailing ship
beneath a windless sky
Nowhere to hide
from the sun that enlightens the day
burns my eyes
and brings water nourishing clouds
to drop it in the poison water
that mocks my thirst
What fish will swim below
I see a gift of life or a drowning abyss
And birds up high tell not their flight
towards gifting shores
or vast migrations
While those planes in distance
out of my reach
and out of their site
and to ships at night
I am only darkness and silence

I am hope when I am happy
and I am sadness when I'm in despair
I am life when I am living
and I am death when I am there

Letter to the curious traveler

The curse of intellect
disguised as a blessing
is an evil temptress indeed

For in my youth,
such a confusing and turbulent time,
I was taught
but not shown
I was prepared to read
but not to understand
I was explained how
but not explained why

and now
I have been shown the understanding of the why
by the most dangerous of human weapons
Curiosity

Oh gentle readers
please do not be frightened by my warning
for curiosity can lead to revelations
of a most wonderful nature
It can show us the path to the moon itself
that watches over us
and guides us
so that we may touch it's aged skin
with a thankful gesture of respect

It could take us inside the minds of ancient philosophers
who's dreams would never reach the heights
of the instant global library
filled with their meager thoughts

In fact
there is nothing
that a curious mind
cannot attain
But curiosity partners
with some powerful and fraudulent allies

Deceit and ignorance smile so welcoming on the misguided
and curious
ready at any moment
to bite with poisonous fangs
of misunderstanding and lies
And temptation
Siren to the week and unworthy
Wields her magic to the ruin of all that fall for her trickery

And though wisdom be a light at the end of the tunnel
the tunnel is just a trick of the light
The deeper down
the hall of knowledge one goes
the farther away the end becomes

So with bravery
and in good conscience
do I use the last arrow of my defense
and launch
it soaring towards from where I came
This letter of warning attached

Beware
the path ahead
for even a glance
in the wrong direction
cannot be forgotten

look forward my fellow travelers
and then look behind
the light back
is much brighter and closer

And I leave you
with a promise of hope
When the light of wisdom
I finally do reach
I will shout back
until my very last breath
not with the paths to choose
but with the ones to avoid

Please listen
so that my journey is not wasted

A voice from the stars

What do my eyes perceive

What image is chosen to make its mark

A myriad of choices each day

that flicker off into obscurity

Will today hold a yellow aster in a field of red

Which voice lost in the wind will find a melodious home

within my song

Which star will cast a spell through the dancing trees to

catch my gaze

A quick glance up is the answer

A message sent before the dawn of dawns

A history of an ancient star

with no Rosetta Stone at hand

There is only wonder

Who is looking up to see our stars reprise.

Who will see the history of this day

broadcast on a gleam of light deep into the future

And are they thinking the same as me

of what miracles do I miss each day

that pass through my eyes

3am demons

I am never more vulnerable, more frightened, then at the 3 AM hour
For in the power of daylight I wield a lifetime of experience as an
unbreakable sword
and I am protected by the unstoppable growing power of wisdom
The world, a pale blue marble in a universal toy box for my amusement
no dangers can penetrate me when I have the answers
I am made of lightning and cry out thunder
Yet the enemy that I hide so deep within need simply wait until I succumb
to human exhaustion
The hidden enemy waiting for the enemy of all to strike

Time
Time is the enemy I cannot defeat
Time marches with the armies of sin, guilt, anxiety, and pain
armies I have trained all too well
And under the cover of darkness and during the vulnerability of peaceful
healing
the demons strike
They attack that which none can protect
the frailty and imperfection of humanity
the conflict and confusion of self
And it is these demons which I must fight with the ultimate weapon of war
Peace
Trapped in the inescapable prison of humanity, caged with demons of
memory
I will make peace in the mirror
and move on

Illusion

I see the moon kiss the horizon
And steal the way into the sky
Shining down on a quiet landscape
Changing colors in a frightening light
I hear the rhythm of a train in the distance
I sense the journey from its fading cry
You wave and smile and call to me
I run to you and hold you tight
In your embrace I feel free
I only wish this was real
Duos prance and triplets swirl
But I can only see the one
Colors dance, project, and swirl
From the white lance of the sun
A bird flies towards Heaven's Gate
Where down is up and up and down
To get there I must live my fate
To crawl to walk in earth to drown
I see through the sky and the ocean is clear
The trees are gold and gray
Rainbows and clouds fill my eyes
The grass stands tall and the buildings sway
The voices speak yet I only hear sounds
My own thoughts lead me astray
The heat feels cold and the ice will burn
I laugh I hope I run I pray
What can I feel what can I see
What can I touch is it part of me
Help me through this delusion
Trapped in a grand illusion

Leadership

Early morning awakens me with the haunting screams of the world in pain
How can I sleep comfortable when I hear a million screams for shelter
I have to protect the world
I have to keep them warm and illuminated in this cold dark winter
A home for those wondering and in sorrow
Let me think
Any home starts with digging the foundation
Curse my human limitations
I can't do it
I can't dig that deep
But I can lay the foundation for my family
And I will
But what of those with no tools and no land
The answer can't be selfishness
I just need to work harder
Dig a foundation to shelter all
I need to dig the Grand Canyon
Wait
That's it
I'll make a foundation the size of the Grand Canyon
But how can I be the Colorado river flowing with determination over
countless years
I can't
Let me think
I am but one fleeting drop of rain in a passing storm, soon to be forgotten
Just one of a million storms that have and will come
So that's what I'll be
I'll be that first drop

Return to forever

A cold awakening breath from the winter wind reveals an ancient insight as
the trees dance to the music of the air
I see the flexibility of all the rhythms of reality
The daily rise and fall of the sun, each day with a different vision
The seemingly eternal message scribed by the stars, edited for each
millennial generation
The ebb and flow of love and sorrow, the price of being human
The all powerful first note of creation
and the unpredictable and inevitable coda

I see music as a reflection of all that's around
not metronomic perfection but a harmonious flowing sound
I hear the flora and fauna in an earthly orchestration
and if I listen enough I feel a peaceful elation
I feel musical virtuosity as a lifelong endeavor
I discover a passionate quest to return to forever

The delusion of night

The days end comes swift and unforgiving

Mental exhaustion creates a weakened body from the

endless daily stream of consciousness

Daylight hours turn into a point of light lost in the

forgotten future

I shelter with the night protected by a blanket of

darkness in the quiet comforting silence

Caught in a frozen cage between the fading past

and an avalanche of possibilities, time becomes a

singularity as memories collide

The air becomes still and I breathe it to life

Shapes turn to shadow

Sounds turn to mystery

and I begin to fade

Armed with the faith of rebirth

I submit to the ether and pass to a new reality

A time traveler at the doors of tomorrow

And the stars look down

Forgotten breath

In the garden of innocent wonder
that's where I make a choice
Deep within the ancient forests
that's where I am found

I try so hard to look back
to remember to re-discover
what has been gone for so long

I plant in tainted soil but it does not last through the winter
I listen to the songs of the wind blow through urban trees
but it is choked by a cancerous growth that spreads out from
the heart of a city like a multilimbed serpent
So I travel
I travel far until the roads end and the cancer can spread no
more
And I walk
and I walk
into a forest so deep that eyes cannot penetrate

and suddenly I can breathe
like I've never taken a breath before
so sweet is the air with the nectar of life
that I'm starting to remember
of a home long forgotten

Andromeda

I awaken in the faint early morning dawn

Birds sing ancient tales, how do I respond

Weaving trees prelude the gentle moonlight

Early morning stars and I wonder what's beyond

I sometimes fade in a wandering crusade

Trying to find balance in all that I know

Scorched from the light I sometimes hide in the shade

And wait for the night to travel long ago

A nearby friend, a princess lost in the sky

Beauty formed from beauty, nomad of the sea

I look to you for answers so far with no reply

Legend of old to immortal by name

Hidden within the family of burning lights

You mystify still we are the same

With ancient metals on a blue shift flight

Our faded path to unite rock and flame

I dream when I look far away

Dreams of hope dreams of curiosity

Dreams to pass and dreams to stay

Sister Sister please connect with me

Andromeda

The fate of all

he deception of present
forward moving constant motion
never stopping always changing
to dream to grasp to dream
one reality billions of perceptions
sometimes changing always destroyed
filling the black hole of history
an endless void endlessly filled
incessant numbers countless lifespans
some fated with early demise
some blessed with longevity
some living to legendary stature
grasping to antiquity
or even wandering in the now
exceedingly drawn toward fiction
cryptic puzzle from times blended mixture
reaching for a mythological peak
fusing fantasy and veracity
fuel for imagination
some with powers derived from power corrupt
to reach a divine position
eventually lost in the forgotten void
a fate inescapable
discovery a narrow chance for salvation
reborn somewhere on the path
a repeated journey
to be lost in time

Awaken to perception

A simple wind to give life
circling the globe
pulsating in and out
from trees to animals
from animals to trees
THE BREATH

Sunlight
The one true visionary
The giver of truth
Mirrored endlessly throughout the night sky
A universal light
THE EYES

Birdsong in the spring air
Thunder in the distance on a summers eve
Leaves under foot on an autumn woodland path
The peaceful silence of snowfall on a calm frozen lake
THE VOICE

I lie in a field
as the soft grass pillows my skin
A gentle rain cleans a hot summer sweat
I walk home and grow tired
at the mercy of the solid ground beneath my feet
and the gravity to hold me tight
Arrival home brings a gentle kiss hello
and a loving shared meal
THE TOUCH

Collective thoughts
Billions upon billions of words
Love
Compassion
Truth
Prayer
Community
Family
Friendship
Devotion
THE MIND

Take life from the breath of God in the air all around
Be enlightened with the eyes of God and behold the truth
Listen to the voice of God and hear the universal symphony
Be blessed by the touch of God in the stories you live each
day
And realize with the mind of God
what heaven really is

Time travel

Why give
a minute to a star
a millennium to a whisper of wind
a season to the Mariana Trench
a forgotten memory to a man

What of
the smile of Cleopatra
star fields before the sun
the tick of a clock
the first interstellar traveler

How long
have the birds sang
has murder been
does a photon live
will humans last

What is
time
but
a flicker of light
the depth of space
lost treasures
another chance

Accept not the senses

Take note of fools who see with their eyes
for their wisdom is flawed through limited site
Beware of the attendant who listens to sounds
and does not grasp the beauty or the meaning

Dangerous are the human senses
not for the imprecise nature of perception
as for the precision of which we accept what we perceive

For what is vision but a view to the past
The view of a moment is of a moment gone
And what is touch but a trick of distance
The space between atoms as is the space between stars

Hear not sounds, but meanings
See not sites, but truth
Feel not matter, but what lies between
Accept not the senses, but question thy self

Air

Why does sound seem clearer
after the rains depart
Why does thought seem so
much more peaceful
I don't want to know
I just want to breathe

Breathe

here's something about the way the rain cleans the air

There must be a scientific way to explain it

But I don't want to know

I just want to breathe deep of the fresh new beginning

Let the cool air renew my lungs

Sometimes I can't breathe deep enough

I want to stare at the trees as they glisten from porch lights

Meditate on tiny rivers down slanted streets as they head

home to the sea creating waterfalls on sewer grates

Even the cars seem to splash through the streets like children

in a summer lake

I can hear them now playing in the distance

Why does sound seem clearer after the rains depart

Why does thought seem so much more peaceful

I still don't want to know

I just want to breathe

Realize the air

Zephyr of life
Angel of energy
Bring me to the garden
with the breath of synergy
Architect of music
Orator of delight
I am at peace from your calm
and enlivened from your might
You surround me with security
Yet I perceive no weight
Protect us from murderous light
Whose colorful beauty you create
With floating seas of the vitality
You appease the worlds thirst
With a cool gentle touch
Or a violent voltaic burst

Please cradle us, prime protector of earth
Please hear our cries of song and sorrow
Please forgive us for our selfish destruction
Please forgive us and bring us to tomorrow

A whisper in the wind

What secrets lay amid the air

the stars may think on quiet nights

I dig for treasure with breath to spare

And watch the birds on joyous flights

They sing a song, an ancient rhyme

and dance among the currents flow

They rest on trees from time to time

and trouble not with those below

I long to touch the painted sky

To grasp the fate at rainbows end

A message sent from sun to eye

To illuminate, to earth transcend

I shout and cheer the racing wind

A whisper vanished in a thunderous sound

A drop below the ethereal sea

An invisible mark on the governing ground

Release your fate to the wind

Cast your fate into the wind my friends and soar into the heavens
Take to the skies like song birds in spring
For the wind knows the way
As the bringer of life, it's sees all and hears all
It romances the gentlest of flowers to dance in the night
and can bring down the tallest of mountains with an endless cycle of
tempest rage
It gives a voice to the trees
or may silence the loudest scream with its might
As I humbly bow down to the majesty of the wind
so does the wind submit to the mercy of the all powerful sun
Born before the world itself, the unceasing sunlight entices the air into an
invisible swirling ballet
Decides it's every movement
Quenches its thirst
and gives color and shape to formless chaos
And as I glance beyond the sun, I see the ultimate power in the universe
The controller of all things
The creator of all form
Unity
For I see the explosion of creation that separated all things
And the desire of unity, the force of attraction, that brought everything
together and created all that we know
And it is attraction that continues to fuel the flames of the sun, and give
breath to the wind
So release yourself to the air
and let its currents guide your flight
and you will be powered by atomic harmonies as old as the dawn of
creation

Symphony

Breath of the world sing loud sing bright

sing to me the tale of tonight

The dancing rhythm of a distant train

The gentle roar of a faraway plane

A single bird on the way to its nest

And a chattering flock overhead on a quest

Distant cars emote and converse all around

The song of tonight seems intent to surround

The wind through the trees help them dance, swing, and

sway

To the symphony of sound sent from wind far away

For the source of this wind simply wait for the dawn

and the music of light with its sunrise baton

Conscious Energy

Memory driven spirit destined
for entropy
I am part of the everything,
I am conscious energy

Return to childhood

As I look for the difference between darkness and light, I realize it is
mythology to the blind
As I look for the difference between wealth and poverty, I discover it has
no meaning to those who are content
I walk alone through my house and see everything I have gathered
There was once a time when all that I possess, I did not
I was happy then, am I happier now?
Interesting phrase alone through my house
When my family returns and I am not alone, house turns to home
As I continue to ponder dawn slowly illuminates through my windows
The things I have bought and gathered, shine as heavy burdening chains
of attachment
My house, my home, reveals itself as a temporary shelter
As mid-morning sun arrives, illumination begs for entrance
I open the curtains and sunbeams dominate the room
Yet it is not the dirty windows, dust filled air, or the floor, warn out for
from years of travel, that is revealed
For I see true treasured possessions as significance of actions and
experience
And I feel my true home with the ones that smile when I arrive
I wonder what more can sunlight offer me
As a turn I see a door
As I open it to my surprise and entire world is on the other side
I step outside and wander around and think what more could there be
Then I look up

Starlight

And despite the dreary and dreamless
I dream
Of future fates on hopeful horizons
Of sailing ships in starfield skies
Through the muddled masses and meticulous machinery
Through the frantic frenzy of hectic humanity
beyond the madness of the maze
I see

because I can't unsee
and I have seen
The human in humanity
The spirit in spirituality
The kind in kindred
The life in wildlife
The song in birdsong
and
the light in starlight

Common Man

I am made from the stars and the planets

Billions of years I took to make
I take power from mountains, and oceans in my veins
Although I sound immortal, oh how easily I break
For I am just a common man, captive in mortal chains

I am blighted with thought, feel, and reflection
An indentured slave to passion, hunger, and drought
I appeal to the mercy of celestial protection
to reveal my potential and remove my doubt

For I have the command of a prophet, I see what lies ahead
I have control of my fate with the mastery of choice
of the straight and familiar or the unknown we all dread
The joy of freedom derives from my hidden voice

I pray for release from the bonds of time and find its latent prize
The constant motion forward from pain and sorrows amassed
Although the curse of memory contains many fading cries
Times healing potency casts pain banished to the past

I am million year old energy, I am the future I envision
I am potential, I am tragedy, I will rise, I will descend
I am conscious energy with the power of free decision
I am humbled with humanity, I am creations end

Evolution

A cloud guarded moon shelters out of sight
As I see the world by a comforting street light
A lonely star cracks the heavens free
And I stare amazed into eternity

I breathe in deep from the ethereal breeze
A gift from an alliance with the slumbering trees
As the ancient air glides on a perpetual flight
That decides the tone on this cold calm night

A mischievous cat on a spirited quest
Runs shadow to shadow as a welcomed guest
At comfort with both the primitive and new
He is balanced between worlds, while I am askew

An animal hiding in a mechanical vision
Long removed from the garden by an ancient decision
I migrate inside to the refuge I keep
And the safety and warmth of a long nights sleep

Crossroads

I only ask for truth but I'm surrounded by lies
Data spread by puppets under a factual disguise
I will not compromise just to rise with blind allies
I will set my eyes on the most magnificent prize
I will unearth the genuine, see the divine, and join the wise

Those with the power keep us in conflict and confusion
They create the fuel for the fight and burn the fire of delusion
Blowing hot air on the flames to create a billion sparks of illusion
Deceit cloaked in deception of well-crafted collusion
To join the distracted masses or live in seclusion This cannot be my only conclusion

Show me the way
I know it's within reach
I don't understand what I see
But who can I trust to teach

Ignorance fed by ignorance packaged with promises and branding
No one is ever wrong, we all believe we are upstanding
Ego and character are always tenacious and demanding
As patience proves humility to be righteous and commanding

We are at a crossroads of growth and evolution
Do I choose the darkness of self persecution or a truthful revolution
If we look away from greedy desire and towards cultural contribution
The truth may appear as a peaceful united solution

Crossroads part 2

How easily fooled and corrupted is the determined mind
For only fools search for confirmation and latch onto the like-minded
The corruption and chaos caused by the illusion of rights and privileges
is like a hate filled fire that spreads violently through the peaceful serene
grasslands
Panic struck animals, innocent of the meaning, stampede for safety
through the flames
sending sparks rising to the air only to fall again and re-ignite
I stand helpless as a spectator crying out to the sky
to the great healing powers of the cool gentle calming rain
Please forgive them, great unforgiving universe, for they are only human,
they know not
who they are

Born from the oceans
raised by the trees
educated from necessity
at the mercy of the tools we create
We find ourselves standing a the crossroads of evolution
with no signs to point the way
Ancient genetic callings clash with arrogant fueled contemplation in a silent
internal battle for the control of direction
7 billion battles
Infinite directions
And only when we question the very ground that we walk on can we ensure
that it is solid and supportive
And only when we venture out into the unknown can we experience the
illumination of discovery
And only together does this work

I am the light

The body matters not when we are connected in spirit
For the body is fleeting on a path of destruction
And the mind is on a connective journey to join the all
The mind is a time traveler with visions of the past and future
A god with the potential to protect or destroy all it sees
A warrior to shield us from the onslaught of perception
It is the essence of beauty when we look without light
Is the destroyer of artistry when drowned in corruption
It is a haven for all things when the doors are open
And it is pure love when we set it free.

One

In the calm and the quiet
In the peace of the night
When light and air are still
As thoughts disappear
As emotions are buried
As I am freed from the restraints
of reflection and perception
It all becomes clear
I see without light
from the radiance of awareness
I feel without touch
embracing universal connections

A global sea of air
Trapping sunlight's glare
Oceans minuscule and oceans great
Land and sky, water will permeate
Beast, flora, rock, earth
Life, action, death, birth
History fading, elusive, and past
Future impending, open, and vast
Stars and planets in infinite space
The universe in reach, ready to embrace

Connection the only truth
Harmony the only sound
Unity the only choice
Everything IS One

Rhythm

Rhythm is everything
Everything is rhythm
From the heartbeat of a hummingbird
To the swirling dance of tangled galaxies
There is a pulse
There is a meter
There is a rhythm
From the precision of a vibrating atom
To the whimsy of a conductors wand
The rhythms of the world synchronize
and become one
crash and are reborn
and fly unencumbered through the freedom of three-
dimensional eternity
I flow with the rhythms and I harmonize
I barricade against a barrage of rhythmic attacks and I absorb
I stand back and observe the rhythmic orchestration of a
universal symphony and I am enlightened with wonder

Chemical warfare

I am the earth, the sun, and the rain
I am carnage for forest and beast
I am the master of all I obtain
The product of a lifelong feast

I am a slave to those before me
With whom I share the same fate
Never really holding the key
I roll the dice and I create

I run scared and I rage with fire
I turn passion into carnal desire
I'm in distress when I know it's not true
Wisdom the only hope of rescue

Temporal presence faded to the immortal
A lifelong journey to an unknown portal
Guided by a self we cannot see
In a time guarded prison we cannot flee

We are the alchemist and we are the test
Conscious energy on a survival quest
A chemical burn with never a rest
Hoping and praying that we are blessed

Monolith of light

DISCOVERY

A call from the setting sun

in the twilight of dancing silhouettes

I see the colors fade to black

and they talk to me

A rainbow sent from a star

splattered across the world

Then I listen

colors speak

only to shatter reality

"I am a trick of light,

for I am not"

"All things exist in the dark,

Except me"

How can something exist only in the light?

I reach out to touch the colors

But it is just a reflection

I can't touch a reflection

No more than I can touch what's inside a mirror

And what is reflected but the sun itself

I listen to this message delivered on beams of light

Oh what a wondrous guide is illumination

DIRECTION

A beacon through the murky waters depth
to behold the grand emergence of the first step
to breathe, to walk, to view the heavens

A glorious sunrise through the distant trees
call to leap from the protective branches
Stand tall
The first step towards the distant lands
The tools of contemplation await
Just reach and grasp

I am awake
I am aware
I am conscious energy
I am ready to see the colors of the world
a reflection of your glory calling me
speaking to me the next great step on the journey
to reflect upon the world
to explore the artistry
to discover
I hear the message
I reflect
What great step will sunlight bring next

Conscious Energy

Memory upon memory thought upon thought
We build and grow ebb and flow
History learned then repeat
Advance or retreat both from defeat
Billions of battles each day and night
Everyone is wrong, everyone is right
Defend your spirit, prepare to fight
Or leave your house to go out in the light

Through my window I see humanity burn
Crashing at each turn unable to learn
Fathers and sons repeating in turn
Find those like us and find them fast
To maintain our faith stay proud, discern
To fade lost in the forgotten past

I am the light I am the dark
an infinitesimal fading spark
I am made from rock and earth
Passion light dust rebirth
Fueled from fire and nourished from death
Crop and carnage for reflection and breath
An infant 1 billion years old
Water carbon acid gold

Memory driven spirit
destined for entropy
I am part of the everything
I am conscious energy

www.ingramcontent.com/pod-product-compliance
Lightning Source LLC
Chambersburg PA
CBHW072128090426
42739CB00012B/3104